Around
Gillingham

IN OLD PHOTOGRAPHS

Around Gillingham

IN OLD PHOTOGRAPHS

Collected by PETER CROCKER

ALAN SUTTON

Alan Sutton Publishing Limited
Phoenix Mill • Far Thrupp
Stroud • Gloucestershire

First Published 1992

A catalogue record for this book is available
from the British Library.

ISBN 0-75090-1993

Typeset in Sabon 9/10.
Typesetting and origination by
Alan Sutton Publishing Limited.
Printed and bound by
WBC, Bridgend, Mid Glam

This is a beautiful place, full of little bridges, rivulets, mills and cottages – and
the most beautiful trees and verdure I ever saw.

(John Constable RA in a letter written to his wife, Maria, when he was staying
at Gillingham as a guest of his friend Archdeacon Fisher, 5 September 1823)

Contrary to the general condition of towns in this part of the county, Gillingham
may be defined as a bustling, thriving, rapidly improving place, with an
increasing population and a future before it.

(Mates, *Dorsetshire Illustrated*, c. 1900)

Contents

Matthews Brewery dray teams lined up and ready to start their rounds. Beer was brewed for over 200 years at Wyke Brewery and their Buffalo trademark was well known throughout the region. The boy on the far right in this 1902 photograph is Dinger Bell (see p. 120). The main brewery building has been converted to residential use in recent years.

Front Cover Illustration
Newbury, with the Royal Hotel on the right, c. 1920. The shop in the middle distance is Bracher Brothers with the sign advertising: house furnishing, cabinet makers, decorators, upholsters and undertakers.

Introduction

The photographs in this volume come from many sources but chiefly from the collection held by Gillingham Museum. The Gillingham Local History Society was formed in the 1950s to promote interest in the town's and surrounding parishes' past, and particularly to find a home for the Freame collection of historical documents, photographs and artifacts that had been left to the safe keeping of the Carter family when the last Freame died. The museum was opened in Church Walk in 1958 and served the town well for over thirty years until it was bulging at the seams and new premises were sought.

One of the most popular features of the displays has always been the photographs. These provide those who remember with a nostalgic peep into their past, and show the young a part of history that they can recognize and to which they can relate. In putting together this book we have also drawn on private collections from within the town and particularly the surrounding villages within the Gillingham postal area.

The quality of the original photographs used varies from near perfect to poor. It would be simple just to reject all the faded, torn or badly focused photographs, but in doing so many of the most interesting subjects would be lost to view. Bear with us and enjoy illustrations such as the shunting horses at Gillingham station and the oldest known local photograph taken in the garden of the Chantry of the 11th Dorset Rifle Volunteers. The 1925 aerial view of Hudson and Martin's sawmills in Station Road and the fair in Victoria Road would have to be omitted if precise focusing were the order of the day. Buildings that have disappeared could not be seen if it were not for the odd amateur image that has turned up.

The pictures are not all particularly old; some have been taken within the last twenty years, but all show the changing face and faces of Gillingham and the area. Many of the pictures used, although very old, are undated and it is a matter of deduction and guesswork to set a time. It is a lesson to us all to mark the date on photographs when they are first developed. The unknown subject of many causes their rejection from this book, although in the case of group photographs the interest can still be experienced even if not all the names are known.

The rich pastures of the Blackmore Vale extend around Gillingham and the chapter on village life contains past, and sometimes long-forgotten, views of peaceful but hardworking communities in the surrounding area that have traditionally looked to Gillingham as a shopping, marketing and social centre. The cattle markets have long gone, but the affinity remains.

Relax and imagine yourself wandering along the main village street shown before you; perhaps the only sounds are the calls of the birds and animals with the occasional horse and wagon passing you. Later years bring the adventure of a motor car chugging by: what a fantastic machine – will it be able to get up Church Hill? All the children run out to look, hoping for a ride. The majesty of the steam traction engines and the quiet hissing power of the steam lorries may be witnessed, the greatest noise being the wheels crushing the stone road surface. The importance of Bourton, with its foundry for making these machines which are exported all over the world, may be felt again.

The artist John Constable was a friend of John Fisher, the vicar of Gillingham in the early 1820s. He visited the town on several occasions during which he painted a number of views of Purns Mill and one of the Town Bridge, as well as making sketches of other subjects. What a shame that the camera was not available to his talent; what a record we should have now of 1820s Gillingham.

The railway which was opened in 1859 has had a great influence on Gillingham and attracted many of the industries and services that caused the town to expand at a steady rate during the second half of the nineteenth century. Most of the buildings that now stand in the principal streets were built from the wealth created by the railway in the late Victorian era.

Many of the pictures show the streets of Gillingham at a time when people could stand and natter in the middle of the road if it suited them. However, most of the scenes are not indicative of the real conditions of life: mud on your boots every time you ventured out on a wet day, and dust everywhere on dry days.

The principal photographers in Gillingham were Charles Johnson for the last part of the nineteenth century, Edgar Samways up until the late 1930s and Ernest Berry for the 1930s and 1940s. Unfortunately very little of Charles Johnson's work has survived and the only pictures included here that can be definitely accredited to him are an early view of the High Street (p. 22) and a studio portrait of Mr E.R. Stickland (p. 108).

Edgar Samways' work was available on many postcards but we are indebted to him for a collection of pictures that he took of less photographed areas of Gillingham, such as New Road, Lodden Hill, Stockwater, Lower Peacemarsh and the Grammar School Footpath, etc. Ernest Berry, who had a newsagents and stationers shop opposite Mr Peach's shop in the High Street, sold many postcards also. When his stock ran low he would pop out with his camera, take a few pictures and run off another batch. This is how so many slightly differing views exist, as postcards were an important means of communication before the telephone was available to all. Rather than writing a letter, people would send a card to say that they had arrived home safely or were coming for tea tomorrow.

Every town in the country played its part in the Second World War. Gillingham and the villages were no different, but very few photographs exist, military or otherwise, from that period. To make up for this you will find in the concluding chapter a selection of aerial photographs of the town showing how the housing developments of the last few years have had a massive impact on the town's environs.

SECTION ONE

In and Around
the Town

The Square at the turn of the century. The buildings on the left are all of the same period and style. The porch in the foreground is that of the doctor's house with Slades department store beyond. The post office door can just be seen to the left of Samways' shop window in the centre.

St Mary's church, 1829. Although a church has stood here since Saxon times it has seen many changes. St Mary's was extensively rebuilt in 1838/9. The only remaining section from the thirteenth century is the chancel. The nave had fallen into disrepair and was not of sufficient size for the growing congregation.

St Mary's church as rebuilt under the guidance of the vicar, Henry Deane. The original chancel now forms part of a larger Victorian church which when first completed had full galleries above the north and south pews. After the First World War a chapel was built adjoining the south side of the chancel in memory of Major Carlton-Cross who was killed in action in France.

William Samways on the step of the pharmacy in the Square, *c.* 1890. The premises were shared with the post office which was entered by a separate door to the left. William was the father of Edgar and Ernest Samways (see p. 75).

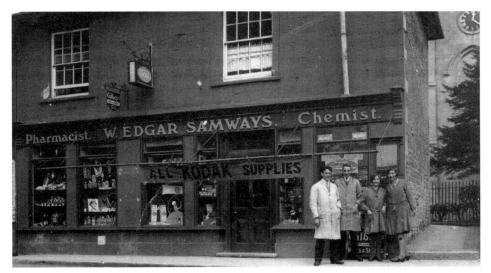

Edgar Samways' shop by the church gate, 1936. Edgar was the man behind the camera for several of the pictures in this book (his photographs can often be identified by the backward sloping captions scribed on the negatives). The staff taking an early lunch break are, from the left: Geoff Coward, Trevor Perrott, Phyliss Martin and Vera Hayter.

Lower High Street from the Square. St Mary's church gate is on the left and the dilapidated box on the wall is believed to have held equipment for the fire brigade. The highlighting of the kerb stones by the Phoenix Hotel to assist drivers helps date the picture to around 1930, when motor car lights were not particularly bright.

The Square after Slades shop was rebuilt, 1904. With its fine Edwardian facade, it looks much the same today as it did then.

The Misses Down's grocery store in the lower High Street was succeeded by that of A.J. Stone. Mr Stone or one of his staff would visit the customer's house during the day to take the order. This would then be delivered by a boy after he had finished school. The shop-front on the right was part of the old Free School (see p. 78).

Wastfield's butchers which was opposite Spring Corner, *c.* 1895. It had its own slaughter-house on the other side of South Street at the rear. The overhanging canopy was used to hang meat out, when the weather permitted.

F.W. Davis's sweet shop by Spring Corner, 1918. This shop was occupied by Senior and Godwin's estate agents business from around 1920 until 1989. Previously it was for several years a watch and clock makers under the names of Bayliss and Aldridge, until it became a confectioners. Standing in the doorway are Mrs E. Taylor and Mrs Stokes, with the owner's daughter Evelyn Davis in front.

Town Mills, *c.* 1910. The Grist Mill on the right with the two half open doors was used for the grinding of corn, wheat, etc. Two quern stones are leaning against the wall by the slit through which the waterwheel could be examined. To the left of the Grist Mill is the Silk Mill, where the silk was separated from the cocoons. It was an extensive building in which dozens of girls worked. This section was built around 1769 and in times of water shortage the Silk Mill had priority over the Grist Mill. The building on the left was used as the silk workrooms and the upper floor was a dormitory for the girl apprentices. Silk milling ceased in 1895 and part of the workroom was used as a printing works before it was demolished in 1924.

Spring Corner. In the wall on the right can be seen a tablet marking the occasion when the first pure spring water well was sunk at this point. The well was a gift of the vicar, William Douglas, in 1802 and served the neighbourhood until 1914 when water was piped in from Mere. The wall has been repaired and lowered in recent years but the tablet and a symbolistic well-head can still be seen.

The Town Mill Leat. This beautiful quiet backwater was bordered on the east (left) by the mill manager's garden which was usually immaculate. Today it is backed by houses at Barnaby Mead.

The High Street from Town Bridge. The newly completed Regal Cinema on the right is in its heyday. This is one of a group of photographs taken from glass plate negatives, rescued from the rubbish cart by Victor Toogood, believed to have been taken by Edgar Samways between 1925 and 1939.

The architect's sketch for the Wesleyan chapel. This is the most imposing feature of the High Street. It was designed by Thomas Hudson and was built in 1876/7. The final result was similar to this but the elevations are more perpendicular and the steeple is taller.

The Red Lion Inn, *c.* 1885. The blank-ended house in the middle distance was also an inn, The Grosvenor, and is now still known as Grosvenor Buildings. A sign on this wall in the 1920s advertised Mr Lawley's Forest Queen Coaches.

S.M. Peach's tobacconists and hairdressers shop in the High Street, 1925. Waverley cigarettes were ten for 3d, Marcella cigars were 3d, 5d or 1s and Turkish cigarettes were available. The shop stayed in business until the late 1950s.

Brice's butchers, opposite the Methodist church, 1914. Mr Gray is on the left and Mr and Mrs Stokes are standing behind their small son Frank. Below is the same shop in 1951. Frank Stokes, now the manager, is still standing outside! The shop is now divided into two, with Chapman, Moore and Mugford occupying one part.

Cheapside House, on the south side of the High Street, 1908, a fine building which still stands. It housed the haberdashery and outfitters business of G. and E.J. Fish and stood opposite to their other shops. When the Fish family sold up, a succession of proprietors (Woodcocks, Wards and Farrells), still in the same trade, occupied the building. The last in the rag trade was R. & A. Stewarts.

Fish's north side premises were on the corner of School Road. This was an unusual building only one room deep, with three doors and curved plate glass windows at each end. The shop was opened here in 1906 and remained in business with the other Fish shops until the late 1920s when Hudson and Martin bought it to use as a builder's merchants showroom. In 1959 they redeveloped the site and incorporated the cottages behind into the present hardware shop and rear yard.

The High Street around the turn of the century. Stedman's on the left was a printers and stationers. Note the wide pavement on the 'Cheapside' and the complete lack of a pavement on the north side.

One of the last traditional cottages in the High Street. Demolished in 1904, it stood between South Lynn and Compton Press. Before the coming of the railway and the redevelopment of the High Street (previously known as part of Newbury), the town consisted mainly of this type of cottage, built of stone and other local materials. In the foreground is the garden of the cottages that stood on the site now occupied by Hudson and Martin's (see opposite page).

Looking down the High Street, 1904. The house on the left is Clive Vale, which was for many years a doctor's house and surgery. Dr Farnfield (father of the solicitor), Dr Alexander, Dr Morse and Dr Jacobs were the main practitioners over the years. In 1983 two shops were 'stuck' on the front which ruined a neatly proportioned Victorian town house.

South Lynn was a major landmark in the High Street until 1978 when it was demolished. South Lynn was built in 1872 by Hudson (later Hudson and Martin) for Mr James Herridge who was reputed to have made his money from selling provisions to the navvies working on the railway. In 1898 Dr Hanley bought South Lynn and added the two rooms on the right, one as a waiting room and the other as a surgery.

Stickland's showrooms, 1939. These were built in 1920. There were workshops to the rear for the repair of agricultural machinery and tractors. Previously a cottage stood on this site (see p. 23). The Morris 10 cwt pick-up truck is priced at £177 10s 0d.

The upper end of High Street with the junction of Station Road on the left and School Lane on the extreme right. The cottage in the right foreground was demolished in 1918, and a garage was built for Stickland's in its place.

G. Pitman, draper, milliner and costumier, is standing proudly outside his shop on the corner of Station Road with his wife, *c.* 1902. The grand address is Paris House. Later the business was purchased by Ayles and Owen, who moved into Station Road after the First World War and took the Paris House name with them.

Station Road from the top, 1904. The post office was built in 1915. The only surviving part of the three-storey premises on the right is now occupied by Hussey's newsagents.

Station Road, looking towards the junction with High Street and Newbury, *c.* 1870. Only eleven years earlier the railway was opened. Bracher Brothers' first shop is on the left. This later became a gents' outfitters and shirtmakers under the name of Edmunds and Stickland. In 1900 the business became Styles (also menswear) until, after a brief sojourn as the Perando restaurant, it changed to the Jukes and Gourlay electrical shop in 1958. All of the buildings in the picture are still standing, with the exception of the wooden and tin barbers shop just right of centre.

Miss S.A. Dunn's High School for Girls, 1903. This was a necessity as the Grammar School did not yet deign to admit girls. In 1906 it came under the control of the head-master and the governors of the Grammar School, but it was not until 1916 that girls were able to attend the same school buildings. This sprawling building on the corner of Buckingham Road was then utilized as a Red Cross hospital during the First World War. Afterwards it became the National Provincial Bank and it is now the Masonic Lodge.

Lower Station Road, *c.* 1910. The sheds on the right formed the frontage of Hudson and Martin's sawmills, and the station yard is in the distance. On the left by the horse and carriage is the saddlers shop (see p. 87).

Newbury from the top of Station Road, 1880s. The School Lane junction is on the left alongside Strange's shoe shop. The little girl in the doorway by the shop is Miss Irene Strange. Richard's chemists is in the building now occupied by Bracher Brothers. It later merged with Herbert's chemists opposite to become Herbert and Richards. The Weare's Temperance Hotel (see opposite) is also advertising itself as a salt store. In the right fore-ground is the Temperance Hall, sometimes referred to as the Town Hall.

The top of Station Road from the west, 1903. Stuckeys Banking Company built their new premises in 1902, on the site of the Temperance Hall. In later years it became the Westminster Bank, and then the National Westminster when they merged with the National Provincial Bank.

The National Provincial Bank on the corner of Station Road, 1928. After the amalgamation with the Westminster Bank this building became the County Library.

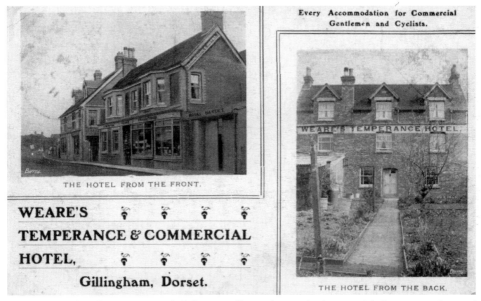

THE HOTEL FROM THE FRONT.

WEARE'S
TEMPERANCE & COMMERCIAL
HOTEL,
Gillingham, Dorset.

THE HOTEL FROM THE BACK.

Temperance hotels were provided for travellers who wished to avoid the temptations of alcohol. This one was at Newbury and was best known for many years as Hughes Bakery. Now it is Newbury Court and has been divided into three shops and several offices.

Barnett's opticians and jewellers in Newbury, *c.* 1930. Alfie Davis is standing in the doorway of this business where he worked and which he later owned.

Lanark Villas in Newbury were one of Bracher Brothers' first building contracts and were built in the late Victorian era.

Fairview Cottage in Newbury was a last moment victim of the internal relief road works when a change of plan necessitated its demolition to make a roundabout at this point. The last occupant was Mrs Cross.

The whole district around Gillingham is full of historic interest, having been the site of many ancient battles.

Newbury from the railway bridge, c. 1910, looking towards the town centre. At this time the north pavement had not been made. All of the buildings on that side are still to be seen. In contrast the south side (left) has been widened and much developed, particularly during the last few years.

H.A. Read's cycle and music shop near the railway bridge at Newbury, February 1932. Henry Arthur Read and his daughter Marjorie (later Majorie Jaggard) are standing on the doorstep. Mr Read had purchased the shop after the First World War and was in business there until 1954.

The parish pump at Ham, 1907. This was situated on the corner of King's Court Road where a pair of semi-detached houses now stand. It supplied water from 100-foot deep springs for those people who did not have their own private wells. There were at least a dozen similar around the town, sunk between 1804 and 1895, although not all had pump-house shelters as here.

Lodden Hill, also known as Popes Hill, is the eastern approach to the railway bridge from Lodden Bridge. It has a third, more official name of Newbury, which commences at the Station Road junction and ends at Lodden Bridge. Vale Cottage on the right is one of the few thatched dwellings remaining in the town. Slades mineral water works occupied the building abutting the footway in the left foreground.

Oldlands Road led at one time from Newbury to Madjeston Bridge, 1930. This part is now generally known as New Road. Its original junction was nearly opposite Hardings Lane and the void created by its amputation was later filled by Newbury House. If the road had been allowed to remain in its 1858 position the railway builders would have had to make two bridges. This was resolved by creating a 'new road' parallel to the railway lines and crossing at the one Newbury railway bridge. The six red brick houses in three pairs are named Pottery Villas and were built in 1912 by the Gillingham Pottery, Brick & Tile Company for their employees. Addison Terrace, on the left, is newly completed.

Prospect House was the home of the Shute family who ran the adjoining butter factory. When Eden Shute's son Reg died in 1981, the whole premises with their extensive garden were sold for development. Prospect Close now occupies the site.

The Sturminster Newton and District Farmers' Dairy stood on the right in 1930. Highnams and later Gillingham Dairies occupied the site which was used as a dairy until the 1980s. This is the new section that gave New Road its name (see p. 33).

The Grammar School Footpath at the eastern end of the old school buildings, 1930s. In 1939 the Modern School was built in the field at the right leaving a green void between the two schools which consisted mainly of a wide ditch or elongated hollow. After the two schools joined as a comprehensive, the hollow was gradually filled over the years and the area taken into school use. When the school was largely rebuilt in 1990–2 the footpath was diverted around the northern perimeter of the school grounds.

Continuing along the Grammar School Path towards Bay, the way was across Mr Ridgley's field to the top of Bay Lane, 1930s. The treescape is no longer to be seen. The elms fell victim to Dutch elm disease and much of the area has been developed leaving little room for trees to survive. The present path rejoins from the bottom right of this field and this old path has now been ploughed and reseeded.

Gillingham Grammar School around the turn of the century. Within the last few years the last of these buildings have been demolished. The school was completed in 1876. Its first pupils were 30 boys and it was 1916 before girls were permitted through its doors.

Elm View Terrace and Bay, 1920. This was a lovely corner of the town which is now much changed. On the right now are Shreen Way and Fairey Crescent junctions, and the hedge is just a memory.

Lodbourne and Lower Peacemarsh, *c.* 1925. This photograph was taken by Edgar Samways and is unfortunately not dated, but was taken before Lodbourne Terrace was built.

It is clear to see why Orchard Road was so named. Mrs Barter is leaning over the front gate of her brand new council house.

The Drill Hall soon after its construction, *c.* 1930. The same view would be difficult now because of trees that were planted along the line of the fence and have since matured. The writing on the door says: '4th Battalion, Dorset Regiment'. This was used for Territorial drills until the 1960s when it became the Youth Centre.

Queen Street from Lodbourne, *c.* 1930. The shop on the left is that of Mere and District Co-operative Society Ltd. It boasted drapery, hardware, furnishings, boots and shoes, clothing and outfitting, and coal departments. The little Austin Seven on the right is parked outside Edward Batho's Garage. The chapel beyond the car was the Primitive Methodist chapel built in 1875. It was used until 1964 when the congregation joined with the High Street Methodists.

Queen Street. The shop in the thatched cottage was Hellewell's sweet and tobacco shop, with Woodcocks next door and beyond that Coles hairdressers.

The Cottage in Queen Street that stood opposite St Martin's. At one time this was a bakers shop with an oven built into a bank at the rear. It was demolished in 1986 when St Anne's Court flats were built. The last occupants were Bert and Elsie Martin.

Chantry Path, 1905. This view from outside Chantry Ford Cottage is no longer possible. The reason is not the hand of man but simply that the trees have grown so that they obscure the panorama.

Chantry Bridge before it was rebuilt. This picturesque scene was spoilt when the river authority decided that the footbridge should be rebuilt in a single span style to avoid impeding the flow.

Wyke Street from Knapp Corner, late 1920s. One could stand in this position up until Christmas 1990 and notice only the smallest of changes. Since that time the 1807 bridge over the River Stour in the middle distance has been replaced and widened, and the road now bears slightly to the right where it meets Le Neubourg Way. In the wall of Chantry Farm on the right the recess of the Wyke Street public parish pump can still be found.

Knapp House, *c.* 1900. This was the home of solicitor Edward Bell for many years in the nineteenth century. The occupier at the time this was taken was either Mr J.R. Anton who left in 1899 or Captain Jackson. For much of the early part of this century it was the home of J.L. Anstruther, JP.

Knapp Corner in Edwardian times. The high wall alongside Wyke Hill is not yet built, nor has the familiar post box been installed. Commonmead Lane is on the left.

Ivy-covered Wyke Hall in a reflective mood. Some of this imposing mansion dates back to the reign of Edward III and other parts are Tudor. In the time of Elizabeth I it was the home of the Cresbyne family. Until the reformation, the house was for a time supposed to have been a monastery, and the lake in the grounds was presumably the monks' fish pond. More recently it was occupied by the Carlton-Cross family. They were responsible for building the chapel of the Good Shepherd at St Mary's church, in memory of their son killed in action in France in 1918. During the Second World War the house was used as a military hospital, then as a depot for Army doctors and later nursing sisters before they were posted overseas. It has now been tastefully divided into smaller dwelling units.

Thorngrove House in Commonmead Lane was built in Victorian times on the site of Queen's Manor. The latter was thought to have been a house for the queens' reception when the kings' visited their palace at King's Court during medieval times. Home of the Peley family, it was used in the Second World War as a billet for American officers and afterwards as a Dr Barnardo's childrens' home. In 1964 the Spastics' Society bought it to use as a residential agricultural work centre. After its extensive modernization and adaptation, the first residents arrived in December 1965.

Part of the Chantry, home of the Freame family, c. 1899. Robert Sadler Freame is standing behind his daughter and wife. They are in front of the only surviving part of the building which is nowadays just discernible in Commonmead Avenue. The portion to the left of the porch has been demolished and is now part of the road.

Stockwater ford and footbridge, *c.* 1929. This is less than one and a half miles from the Square, yet, when shown this picture, four out of five local people are unable to place the scene. The building on the left is part of Stock Farm. Stock Lane only services fields but a footpath goes through to Langham Lane.

St George's church, Langham. This is possibly the only thatched church to be built this century in England. It was the idea of Alfred Manger who lived at Stock Hill House. He intended to build a church on his land for the benefit of the hamlet of Langham and his employees living on the estate. Then the First World War broke out and his youngest son, Lieutenant J.K. Manger, his nephew, George Bredon Kitson, and son-in-law, Captain R. Lancaster (father of Sir Osbert Lancaster the cartoonist), were all killed in action. Before he could give effect to his plans, he himself died in 1917. His widow arranged the consecration of the ground by the Bishop of Salisbury and he was buried in the spot he had chosen to build his church. After the war the Manger family were able to build this church over the grave of Alfred Manger and his wife Elizabeth Ann who had died in 1919. Services are only held now at festivals and special occasions.

Village Life

The wedding of the Revd Arundel, curate of Stour Provost, and Miss Capel-Cure, the rector's daughter, at Stour Provost, 1911. The bridegroom in morning dress is seen arriving at the church. It was a sweltering day necessitating the use of umbrellas as parasols.

The bride, now Mrs Arundel, entering an Austin as the couple leave for their honeymoon. The road is decorated for the happy occasion which the whole village seems to have attended.

The buttermaking classes at Woodville School, 1893. This must have been the forerunner of adult education.

East Stour Crossroads, *c.* 1905. The AA man is Mr House. On the left, standing in front of the original post office, is Mr Fowles the postmaster, holding one of his children. Another daughter, Edith, is one of the two girls standing on the corner. Mr Compton is the gentleman on the right by the Sturminster turning. Shaftesbury is straight ahead with Gillingham to the left.

Fernhill, East Stour, 1920s. The home of Bessie and Katy Martin, schoolteachers, is on the right.

Building workers at East Stour. The subject and place of this pre-1914 photograph are not known, but the men are the staff of W. Fowles of East Stour, who appear to be demolishing a cottage. One from left is Bob Moore, Teddy Watts is fifth from left, and George 'Kippy' Moore is third from right. Fowles were the builders of Addison Terrace in Gillingham.

Browns Lane at the turn of the century. This is still a tranquil area but many of the trees have disappeared.

The Bishop of Salisbury leaving East Stour School, 10 April 1908. He had been in the village to consecrate an extension to the churchyard.

East Stour Church of England School, 1906. The infants' class was at the right end of the building. The remainder were taught in the big room under the bell, which was divided by a curtain. At the time when Harry Hunt and Edith Myall attended, just a few years after this picture, there was no master. Their teachers were Katy Martin, Miss Kalcher and Miss Anning.

The shop at West Stour kept by John Lodder, *c.* 1907. This is on the junction of the main A30 road and the village street.

The road to West Stour from East Stour. Later this became the busy A30, but in 1899 the hunt was able to saunter along unhindered by traffic. The photographer would have been standing near the junction with Head Lane and looking west.

The Ship Inn at West Stour. This was built in 1750 and was a traditional coaching inn. The man standing on the doorstep is thought to be Horace Marvin, the landlord in 1910.

Factory Mill, Fifehead Magdalen, 1903. The mill, photographed by Bertram Freame, was pulled down the following year.

The Fifehead Magdalen Football Team, *c.* 1930. Back row, left to right: George Dowding, Len Dowding, Eric Hopkins, ? Takle, Sid Gray, Frank Gallimore (postmaster at Fifehead Magdalen and clerk to Kington Magna Parish Council). Front row, left to right: Eric Dowding, Charlie Raymond, Stanley Raymond, Howard Rowland, ? Clark, Bert Cox. The team had just won the McCreery Cup at Inwood, Yenston.

Tom and Ada Hayter with Gladys at Pleck, Kington Magna, 1906.

Kington Magna Rectory, *c.* 1912. The occasion is not known.

The pond at Kington Magna Rectory, with the Revd F. Llewellyn Edwards and his goat Jeremiah.

The village shop and bakery at Kington Magna, *c.* 1911. This was kept by Frank Cockerell. Leslie Cockerell is the larger of the two children standing in the doorway. The 1d monsters advertised on the sign are thought to be huge bottles (holding about a quart) of fizzy lemonade.

Kington Scoutagettes at Gillingham Carnival, 1913. This picture was used as a Christmas card by the Rector, the Revd F. Llewellyn Edwards. Girls, left to right: Nellie Raymond, Verna Dowding, Matilda Raymond, Lena Dowding. First boy to the right of the girls: Arthur Stokes.

The bottom of Church Hill at Buckhorn Weston. The Stapleton Arms is the building at the centre on the right with the elegant porch.

Mayday celebrations at Buckhorn Weston School. From the clothes the event is thought to be shortly before the First World War.

Eccliffe Mill was nearing the end of its useful life in 1903. The miller at the time, Jacob Drewitt, who was also a lay preacher, left in 1905.

Putting in the girder bridge at Eccliffe Mill, 1902. The gentleman in the boater is Mr A. Barnes. The old bridge in this position had been sketched by John Constable.

The Red Lion at Bourton with the Slate Club sitting outside, 1878. The landlord at the time was Mr Jeffery. This inn was an important staging place for coaches and commercial wagons during the eighteenth and early nineteenth century since Bourton was on one of the London to Exeter routes.

The old post office at Bourton, 1920. This shop-front was an extension to the front of the cottage behind. It was run for many years by the Lush family. In 1965 the building was demolished, as the post office had moved across the road.

Seth Suter at the junction of the West Bourton and London roads. He was head gardener at Silton rectory for many years. The cottage in the background had been burned down and was demolished in the 1890s.

The Bourton Poachers is the appropriate title for this group of lads, *c.* 1916. Left to right: Jack Suter (holding the rabbit), Ted Long, Ted Fricker, Cyril Long, Maurice Fricker. They are at Easton Place on the path to Queen Oak.

The Round House on Bourton Bridge. This odd-shaped house was in fact a toll-house as well as an undershod mill where edge tools were made in an integral workshop. In 1900 it was demolished, having fallen into disuse.

Looking west from Bourton Bridge. The farm buildings in the middle distance are part of Ivy Lodge Farm.

The female staff at Hindley's Bourton factory, c. 1916. The occasion for the gathering is unknown, but they all seem contented. At one time the foundry employed over 200 people.

Bourton Foundry, 1885.

Hindley's staff outing on one of their own steam lorries, *c*. 1905. Hindley machinery and steam engines were built at Bourton Foundry. Mr Devenish, the manager, is standing in the foreground at the foundry. The vehicle is one of their 'light delivery vans' and is described in their contempory catalogue as being 'designed for loads of one to two and a half tons. It is speeded up to eight to ten miles per hour, and is easy to manoeuvre. The mechanism is so extremely simple that any man of ordinary intelligence can drive it after a short tuition. The boiler is of the Hindley's and Bretherton's patents locomotive type of improved design. The engine has compound cylinders and splash lubrication. For transmitting the power from the engine we employ steel machine-cut gear wheels and roller chain of best quality. Any style of body can be fitted to suit users requirements.'

The road west from Bourton Bridge, *c.* 1910. The Round House on the bridge is gone. The cottage beyond is where the Misses Farthing, who were schoolteachers, lived. The houses in the distance are Orchard Cottages.

Bourton Prize Band. At one time the band contained eighteen members with the surname of Suter, but this is an earlier team, only a few of whose names are known. Back row, left to right: Arthur Suter, -?-, ? Bannel, -?-, Frank Markey, Billy Hosmar (schoolteacher). Seated row, far right: Walter Suter.

Lower Silton, formerly The Rookery. The house was visited by the poet William Blake, writer of the Women's Institute hymn, 'Jerusalem'. He is reputed to have painted some of his 'strange murals' on the walls of one of the sitting rooms.

Alfred Bell, famous as a stained glass window artist, was born in Silton in 1832. He and Richard Clayton formed the company of Clayton and Bell and were responsible for stained glass in the cathedrals of Truro, Durham, Rochester, St Edmundsbury, Gloucester, Hereford and Lincoln, as well as in Bath Abbey and St George's Chapel, Windsor. Bell also designed the choir vault at Sherborne Abbey. At Queen Victoria's express wish, his firm carried out the decoration of the Albert Memorial.

Alan Harris from Manor Farm, Silton, off to the war. His horse went with him to Gallipoli where it was shot from under him. Alan brought one of its shoes home and hung it in Fred Vincent's forge at Milton, where the horse had always been shod.

Harvesting the mangolds on Manor Farm, Silton.

Cottage at Huntingford occupied in 1912 by Mr and Mrs Nash and their four children. It is reputed to be a squatter's cottage, but is more likely simply to be the site of a squatter's cottage. The building has been demolished but the adjacent whitewashed house survives.

An important wedding in Huntingford. Mabel Fricker and Harry Caddy make the union of two local farming families. The reception is taking place at Huntingford Farm.

St Simon and St Jude's church at Milton on Stour. When built in 1866 it had no spire. This was added in the 1890s.

Interior illustrations in Milton on Stour church. These were painted soon after the church was built. In the early 1900s they were painted over on the insistance of the wife of one of the local gentry.

Unveiling of Milton war memorial, 1921. The memorial contains eleven names from the First World War and one from the Second World War.

A Victorian wedding at Milton. Front row, third from left: the bridegroom's mother, Sarah Hull. Front row, centre: the bridegroom, Francis Hull. Back row, far right: William Hull (in top hat), Fred Vincent (in bowler hat, below William Hull). Middle row, far right: Elsie Pond (standing).

Feltham's wheelwrights works, School Lane, Milton on Stour. Apart from wheels the works made a variety of carriages and very good strong farm carts.

The road without a name at Milton on Stour. Littlemarsh, Bourton Road and Post Office Road are some of the names that Milton folk use for this road, but no one seems to know its official title, if indeed there is one.

People of the Town

The servers at St Mary's with the vicar, *c.* 1949. Left to right: Les Dunning, Geoff Wiles, Michael Rose (seated), Bob Carter, John Bracher, Revd E.L. Seager, Ivor Scammell, Doug Burt (Seated), Dennis Hannam, John Fricker.

Robert Sadler Freame and Mrs Freame in the garden of the Chantry, 1898. Mr Freame was a solicitor in the practice of Bell and Freame, which later became Freame, Light and Wylde. For forty years he was clerk to the magistrates of Sturminster Newton, Shaftesbury and Gillingham. A leading citizen of the town, he was at one time chairman of the Grammar School governors, an alderman of Dorset County Council and Deputy Steward of the Manor of Gillingham.

Cook, Ellen and Fanny taking a breath of fresh air, and looking over the chicken run at the Chantry. Fanny (far right) was Miss Young, but of the others we know no more than that they were posing for their employer's son, Bertram Freame.

William Read and his family, 1888. William was a Methodist lay preacher. His trade was picture framing which he carried out at Peacemarsh Stores. Back row, left to right: Minnie, Ellen (Kate on lap), William (Henry on lap), Clara, Adelaide (later Mrs Lampard), Lily. Front row, left to right: Alexander, Martin Luther, Garnet. Adelaide ran a tea and fish & chip shop in St Martin's Square, known recently as Corbins.

The Dorset Yeomanry Ball at the Market Hall, *c.* 1910. Major Freame, the commanding officer, is in the left foreground. The Market Hall was the centre of entertainment in the town during the early part of the century. A cheese market was held here on market days and general auctions on other occasions. It was also Walford's Electric Palace cinema and a theatre but was demolished in the early 1960s.

The British Red Cross Senior Club celebrating its first birthday at the Blackmore Vale rooms, 1950. These rooms were above Slades in the Square. Back row, left to right: G. Hunt, Revd Buckley, Mr Chubb, Mr A. Court, T. Hull, -?-. Front row, left to right: Mrs Hunt, Mrs Collis, Mrs Gray, -?-, -?-, -?-, -?-, -?-, Mrs Musselwhite, Mrs Herridge, -?-, Mrs Hull.

The Venerable the Archdeacon of Dorset, when off duty, was always accompanied by his St Bernard. Edward Leslie Seager became vicar at St Mary's in 1946, was a governor of several local schools, an enthusiastic scout supporter and, as an ex-military man, was chaplain to the British Legion until his retirement in 1979. He was the last vicar to live in the large Victorian vicarage which is now part of Rawson Court.

Ernest Rowsell Samways, MPS, 1885–1986, was born in Gillingham and studied to become a pharmacist. Although he did not return full time to the town until 1936 when his elder brother retired, he worked until 1964 to complete a career of sixty years. During the Second World War he kept the keys to the church tower, ready to ring the bells, day or night, if the Germans landed. In his retirement he wrote a novel, *Dorset Barnaby*, based on his boyhood and giving an insight into Victorian and Edwardian life in Gillingham. He had been head boy at the Grammar School, a parish councillor, school governor and president of the bowls club.

Gillingham pub landlords get their long service awards. On the left are Mick and Muriel Taylor of the Dolphin Inn, and previously the Phoenix Hotel. The centre couple are Mr and Mrs Albert Rose of the Buffalo Inn. Seated on the right is Reg Thorne of the Queen's Head. Standing behind are Franey Matthews and Edward Woodhouse, directors of Hall & Woodhouse Brewery.

A.F.H.V. Wagner, MA, Deputy Headmaster of Gillingham School. Mr Wagner joined the school in 1931. At his retirement in 1969 he was the head of the history department. He is noted for having written a history of St Mary's church and of Gillingham Grammar School, among other minor works. Much of his short retirement was spent in researching a history of Gillingham. This was incomplete at the time of his death in 1971.

Gillingham Floral Decoration Society, 1955. Left to right: Mrs Heane, Mrs E. Reid, Mrs M. Hughes, Mrs H. M. Crocker, Mrs Lanham, a visiting demonstrator, Mrs R. Martin, Mrs E. Martin, Mrs M. O'Dea, Mrs Hull.

Children boating on the river, probably on the mill leat. This stretch was used on Church Fete days particularly, as the vicarage gardens, which are now car park, backed on to the river. This photograph was taken by Mr William Jukes, a Gillingham man who set up a photographic studio in Wilton in 1896.

Charles Howe wearing the town mayor's chain. Gillingham did not have a mayor until the local government reorganization in 1976. Charles served as mayor for the years of 1980 and 1981. Later, he was best known as a local historian and publisher of *Gylla's Hometown*, a colloquial history of Gillingham. He lived and worked in his family building business in Gillingham all his life, apart from wartime service as a pilot in the RAF. Charles also served as a district and county councillor. He died in 1985 at the age of 61.

First World War group of Wyke School pupils. The school was closed in May 1942 and merged with the School Road school. However, Gillingham's expanding population caused a new primary school to be opened in Wyke in 1991. Seated row, second from right: Elsie Lloyd.

The pupils and teachers of the Free School, *c.* 1870. This is at the rear of the school which backs onto South Street, or Back Lane as it used to be called. It could possibly be a last memento before the school moved to the new premises in 1876.

Boys' class at School Road Board School, *c.* 1894. This is the earliest known photograph of the primary school pupils. The Board school was built in 1875 for 110 boys and 110 girls. Front row, third from left: Henry A. Read (see p. 73).

Girls' school at School Road Board School, 1905. The sexes were separated at this time. Third row back, far left: Florence Jane Murch (later Florence Read).

PT for the third form at School Road Primary School, 1952. Top, left to right: -?-, John Hall, Christine Watts, -?-, Joy Jefford, Lyn Trainor, Malcolm Jefford, -?-, Teddy Read. Others include: Francis Martin, Derek Gatehouse, Patrick Allard, Terry Hillier, Susan Raymond, Sue Perkins, Valeen Ayres, Hilary Parker, June Pitman.

The class of 1953/4 at School Road Primary. Back row, left to right: Sam Braddick, Shirley Flower, Rachel Greenland, Margaret Pitman, Margaret Gould, Jennifer Shawcross, Anne Denslow, Michael Dacre, Miss Westerman (headmistress). Middle row, left to right: David Fry, Roy Palmer, Richard Read, Richard Gould, Audrey House, Robert Minshull, Pearce Martin, Jennifer Williams, Margaret McNally, Roger Lydford. Front row, left to right: Timmy Suter, Graham Cook, Phillip Hatch, Roy Whitehead, Maureen Belgin, Christine Cadman, Andrew Dunn, Richard Phillips, Anna Day, David Lloyd.

Industry and Transport

Two of P.O. Baker's hire cars ready for a wedding, 1920. Baker's started in business in 1912 as a posting house and horse-drawn taxi service. Originally the business was in Station Road on the opposite side to their present garage. These Model T Fords were their first motor vehicles. Jimmy Downs is on the left and Walter Hunt is on the right. The taxi business continued until the 1970s when the company decided to concentrate on their expanding motor business selling Rootes Group, and later Talbot and Peugot cars.

The Phoenix brake setting off to Larmer Tree grounds for one of the annual pageants, *c.* 1880. The driver is 'Woodpecker' Maidment. Syd Gatehouse is standing in front at the left. The man with the clerical hat and eyeglasses on his coat is Mr W.W. Slade. His business premises are in the Square in the background, advertising 'china, lamps, hardware, ironmongery and house furnishing'. The Phoenix Hotel is on the left. Note that the windows, bricked up to avoid window tax, have been painted to match the real windows.

The Sorrell family on an outing. The wagonette is at the Knapp Corner end of Browns Lane, East Stour. Mr and Mrs Sorrell are in the front, with Miss Edith and Mr Arthur behind.

Wilfred Chubb in St Martin's Square. He worked for Allard's of Lodden Farm. The 'dung pot' cart was made by Feltham's of Milton (see p. 70).

The milkman in St Martin's Square. The horse and cart carried a fifteen gallon churn of milk, and was the forerunner of the milk-float. The householders had to provide their own containers for the milk to be decanted into. A set of goverment stamped measures of half pint, one pint and quart were carried by the milkman.

A horse-drawn mower at work on H.J. Allard's farm at Woodwater. Henry Read is the man in the driving seat.

Town Mills, 1954. Mr Wedlake is on the right checking that all is well. The ground corn is being slid down to be loaded on the covered truck, while at the left a load of corn is being unloaded onto the platform ready for milling. The mill house is at the extreme right of the picture.

T.H. Brickell and staff on the back waterwheel at Town Mills, c. 1910. From left to right: Tom Brickell, Reg Bridges, -?-, Len Crew. Below: Bert Brickell, grandfather of the present generation who manage T.H. Brickell (Blackmore Press). Printing started in the old Silk Mill workrooms in the late 1890s and continued there for over twenty years. The Brickells then moved to Newbury.

The largest oak cut down and sawn up by Hudson and Martin, *c.* 1922. This is believed to be one of the last oaks from Gillingham Forest.

Hudson and Martin's steam engine, *Sir John French*, with timber carriage by Braddick's field in Station Road in the early 1920s. Left to right: Bert Meatyard, ? Silcox, -?-, Art Hull.

A breather for two sawyers at Hudson and Martin's Station Road sawmills. The long poles with iron ends are for turning the trunks over. A timber dog is being held by the man on the right.

Reg Coward at work in his saddlers shop. For over forty years from 1919 Reg was a familiar sight in Station Road. This shop, with its distinct leather and oil aroma, was attached to the front of his house (lately used as Lawford's electrical shop). When Le Neubourg Way was constructed in 1991, the shop was demolished to make way for the intersection with Station Road.

Experimental helicopter mail services were conducted by the Westland Aircraft company in Somerset and Dorset, seen here in the field adjacent to the football field in June 1948. Westland-Sikorsky and Bell helicopters were used over a route: Yeovil, Sherborne, Gillingham, Blandford, Wimborne, Poole, Wareham, Weymouth, Dorchester, Bridport, Lyme Regis and back to Yeovil.

Gillingham Gas and Coke Company gasholder, 1980. The company was formed in 1837. The adjoining road appropriately became Gas Lane. Gas was produced here for the town, and later for Shaftesbury, until 1970 when North Sea gas was piped in. This picture was taken shortly before the last gasholder was demolished.

A delivery for the Malt House at Bay, *c*. 1905. Towing two four-wheeled wagons posed a difficult manoeuvering problem for the traction engine. It seems that Charlie Maloney took the whole family on this trip.

Charlie Maloney, Gillingham's entrepreneur, sitting in the cab of a 1906 Hindley steam wagon, 1910. He was a coal merchant, corn and feed merchant, engineer and glue manufacturer in Station Road. The coal was the prize at the carnival.

The Light family with their Gillingham-made 'Magnet' bicycles, c. 1907. Left to right: W.H. Light (founder of W.H. Light and Company), Betty Light (later Curtis), Mr Evill (father-in-law), J.H. (Hacker) Light, Mrs W.H. Light. W.H. Light, who was a saddler by trade, started manufacturing bicycles at his Peacemarsh home in 1897. In 1910 the works moved to the Newbury site, where Light's Garage is now.

Light's Garage as it was, 1930s. By this time motor cycles were their main business. The premises stayed much the same until 1956 when a pull-in filling station and a showroom were built.

Gillingham and District Modern Laundry worked from the old United Dairies building in Station Road, where P.O. Baker now store and clean cars. The artwork on this 1951 van was painted by Eddie Feltham who worked for Stickland's for over forty years. The lady's escort was waiting in white tie, top hat and tails on the other side of the van.

Employees of Gillingham Pottery, Brick and Tile Company making bricks, 1891. The town is established on a thick strata of Kimmeridge clay, which is ideal for brickmaking. The business was founded in 1866 alongside the railway to allow easy access to its customers. The small boy in the pantaloons is Mr J. Webber of Tomlins Lane.

The brickyard staff outside the blacksmiths shop, 1875. The tall building was the pottery. The chimney served the boiler. Of the staff of seventy, only one appeared to be a white collar worker.

Digging clay by hand for bricks during the First World War. These men were digging at the brickyard to the west of the East Stour road. Far left: Charlie Francis. It was not until the late 1930s that a tunnel was bored under the road to enable clay to be dug from the east side of the road in the area which is now the much admired fishing lakes.

A new boiler for Gillingham Pottery, Brick and Tile Company, *c.* 1928. The boiler was delivered by Hudson and Martin's steam engine, *Jellico II*. Behind the engine is a stack of drain pipes.

Slades mineral water works. This sign can still be seen as you pass along Newbury east of the railway bridge. It must have been good paint as the works closed in 1920! They made a variety of lemonades, ginger beers, etc. in glass bottles which used a captive glass marble as a stopper.

The Station Yard on market day at the turn of the century. The farmers and dealers parked their carts and carriages at the South Western Hotel. Staff at the hotel took care of the horses. The market was at the rear of the hotel. The wagons on the left are parked outside Oake Woods bacon factory. Market days (Mondays until 1939, then Fridays) were busy, bringing good business to most traders in the town. Buyers came by train to bargain for produce for other parts of the country, particularly London. Other users of the South Western Hotel were the commercial travellers who also arrived by rail. They stayed for a few days, hiring a pony and trap to visit the neighbouring towns and villages to show samples and seek orders. On the extreme right, the large barn-like building is the Market Hall (see p. 73).

The cattle market, Station Road, from the station gates, 1890s. The market was operated by Senior and Godwin's who were in business in the town as estate agents and auctioneers. They closed Gillingham market in the late 1950s and concentrated their efforts at Sturminster. At the time of this picture, the buildings all look newly erected. The farmers are hanging around using the day as a social event, just as much as a business occasion.

The Balch family and dairy staff at Slodbrook Farm, Milton, *c*. 1920. The equipment is mainly for cheesemaking. William Balch is standing behind the cheeses on the table with his wife, Agnes, to the right of him. Around this time one of their daughters, Hilda, had a National Dairy Diploma for instructing on cheese and buttermaking on farms all over Dorset.

Staff at Salisbury, Semley and Gillingham Dairy, Station Road, 1906. Later the dairy became part of the Wilts United Dairy company based at Trowbridge. At this site, now known as Somdor House, the dairy acted as a collection depot. Milk was purchased from the small farmers who produced only a few churns each day. The milk was then distributed, either by direct sale or by train to dairies in London.

The end of haymaking at Compton Stud, Sandley, *c.* 1900. Note the very wide hayrake – no wonder they look so relieved to have finished building the rick! The owners of the Stud at this time were Captain William Henry Fife, JP and Captain Phipps-Hornby, JP.

Mr Peter Burrell, manager of the National Stud, taking delivery of his new black Riley Pathfinder. This picture was used as publicity for the British Motor Corporation in 1957. The National Stud at Sandley was relocated from Ireland at the end of the Second World War. It was the cause of several informal visits by Her Majesty Queen Elizabeth II to inspect her horses.

The Compton Press printing works, situated in the High Street nearly opposite School Road, *c.* 1910. The press published the *Three Shires Advertiser*, a local newspaper. In 1920 the business was acquired by Prideaux of Motcombe to produce advertising and packaging material for their dairy and bacon trade. The building was demolished in 1966. The site is now part of the South Lynn Centre occupied by an estate agent and Chris Hussey's sports shop.

The manager's house at Oake, Woods and Company, decorated for the coronation of Edward VII. The original shop was a lean-to on the right. Later the main factory front was built on this site.

Oake, Woods factory towards the end of its working life. Founded in 1847, and by far-sighted planning built in the railway yard, the factory was for a great many years the major employer in the town. It was renowned for its bacon products which, with the coming of the railway, were sent all over England. It finally closed in 1985.

A familiar sight in the area during the 1950s and 1960s. These Oake Woods one-and-a-half-ton Morris Commercial PV vans were painted with the lower half in maroon and the top in cream with maroon signwork by Eddie Feltham of Stickland's Garages. The two back doors had a packet of sausages painted on them. Each time a new van was ordered, a sample pack of sausages was sent up to Mr Feltham. These were cooked on the workshop stove and happily consumed by the staff.

A grand produce display for the carnival. Dennis Sharp is in the white coat on the left and 'farmer' George Francis is taking a ride in the 1953 carnival.

Eden Shute's butter factory in New Road. In this building various dairy products were produced, most famously Eden Shute's Golden Melon brand butter. The business was sold out to Aplin and Barrett in the late 1930s. During the Second World War the factory was used as the Air Raid Warden's headquarters.

Dr Hanley's new car was a 10-12 hp Humber four-seater tourer in dark green and black. It was supplied by Stickland's and first registered on the 7 February 1906. It is pictured in the driveway of South Lynn where he resided and had his surgery. In the background on the right, on the opposite side of the High Street, Fish's shop is in the course of construction (see p. 22)

The first motor car in Gillingham. The registration number BF 89 was owned by Mr E.R. Stickland. When registration numbers were first required, from December 1903, Dorset was perhaps unfortunate in being issued with the BF series of letters. By the time the number BF 162 was reached the motoring public had said they were not going to be labelled a BF! Dorset was issued with an alternative set of letters, FX. Owners of BF vehicles were able to change to FX if they applied to the County Council. BF 89, a dark green and black Humberette with Dog-cart body, registered on 4 January 1904, was not changed.

Hine Brothers' first steam engine, a Burrell Gold Medal steam tractor, during the First World War. Left to right: -?-, Bill Hine, Jack Hine. Hine Brothers were engaged on Government war contracts in both the First and Second World Wars.

The Hine brothers with their father, 1944. Left to right: Edward Hine, H. Hine senior, Jack Hine, William Hine. The sign behind denotes the company's position as the local unit of the emergency wartime transport organization.

Excavating for a new filling station in front of South Lynn, 1959. The Ford Thames Trader and Ruston-Bucyrus excavator belonged to Hine Bros, subcontractors to W. Howe & Son who completed the works. In 1918 Mr Jack Stickland had bought the house and grounds to use as a residence and offices. Eventually it was surrounded by the trappings of a buzzing business (see pp. 107–112).

Neville and Haines engineering business at the Lodbourne end of Queen Street, 1920. Before 1930 Mr Batho bought the premises which always had associations with the motor or motor cycle trade until 1989. Then A303 Tyres sold the land for redevelopment.

Woodcocks at Cheapside House. Woodcocks started at the top of Wyke in the grocery trade in a shop on the town side of the terraced cottages. They moved to Newbury (drapery and boots) next to the bicycle shop. Then in 1918 the business moved to Queen Street. Mrs C. Woodcock advertised drapery and millinery and Mr C. Woodcock advertised carpentery, joinery and wallpapers. The drapery store moved to Cheapside House in around 1930 while a menswear business remained in Queen Street.

Tailors at work in Shephard Brothers Shop at the Barton, Queen Street, 1902. Arthur Shephard is seated cross-legged on the bench.

The High Street and Stickland's site, as it was in 1963. At the centre bottom is the School Road junction and the library can just be seen at the left edge. The Victorian house in the centre facing School Road is South Lynn (see p. 24), with the large pale roof of Stickland's car workshop to its rear. The River Stour is meandering around Chantry Fields at the top right, and the square tank adjacent is part of the sewage pumping system. Hudson and Martin's sawmills are at the top with Buckingham Road running left to right just below. In Buckingham Road are Baker's garage on the left and the Coronation Club (end-on to the road between the houses). Much of the centre of this area, from High Street to Buckingham Road, was redeveloped into Gateways and the South Lynn Centre in the mid-1980s.

Edwin Roberts Stickland (1853–1911) was born in Milborne Port, the elder son of a family of nine. He was apprenticed to an ironmonger at Bruton and later in a similar trade in Hereford. Subsequently he worked in Birmingham where he married. In April 1882 he came to Gillingham, where one of his brothers was a shirtmaker in Station Road. Here he opened an ironmongery and smithy business in the High Street on 12 April 1882. On his first day's trade he only managed to take 7s 5d from three sales: a bucket and nails at 4s 9d, a mouse trap at 1s and a hoe at 1s 8d.

Edwin John Stickland (1880–1952), son of the above, had ambitions to become a doctor but lack of money meant that in 1896 he had to join the family business. Under his influence the company saw its greatest expansion. Sticklands were appointed repairers to the Cycle Touring Club, and agencies were gained in Raglan, Royal Enfield, Singer, Rudge Whitworth and Humber Cycles. The motor trade was entered with increasing momentum. He became a leading figure in the local motor industry and remained in control of the firm until his death.

Stickland's ironmongery shop, displaying a wide variety of stock, 1921. Hanging above the doorway are frying pans with more stew pans in front of the second window. Milk churns, which would have been made on the premises, and a wooden butter churn are also on show. The display was set out each morning and left out during the hour-long lunch break during which the shop was shut. Needless to say, all the stock got thoroughly dusty and soiled, but was never pilfered! The telephone number painted on the glass is 4. It was preceded by Samuel Bishop of the Fir Tree public house who advertised 'Cars for hire. Purveyors of petrol, oil and carbide,' and whose telephone numbers were 1 and 2. The number for Freame Light and Wyld, Solicitors of the Square, was Gillingham 3. This is the only part of the original firm still owned by the family. It is run by E.R. Stickland's great grandson, Peter Crocker, and his wife, Glynis.

The shoeing forge and blacksmiths shop of Stickland's, shortly after its aquisition and repainting, 1906. B.P. Edwards was the previous owner of this ironmongery and farriers business which was a rival to the Stickland concern. However, owing to a little trouble with the ladies, Mr Edwards knocked on Stickland's door late one Saturday evening with the offer to sell him the business, stock and premises, provided he could come up with the money before Monday morning. Realizing the strong position that he was in, Edwin Stickland got a bargain price and spent the whole of Sunday in a pony and trap visiting his relations, mainly farmers, collecting the cash.

January 1st 1954

A special day for Stickland Garages, 1 January 1954. Since the end of the war new cars had been in very short supply time as most were sent for export. This was the first occasion that several vehicles were available at once. From left to right, the new owners were to be: Morris Cowley van, Mr J.J. Garrett; Morris Six, -?-; Morris Six, H. Bourne of East Knoyle; Morris Oxford, W. Hurley; Morris Oxford, T. Ayles of Maiden Bradley; Morris Oxford, Mr Walters of Yeovil; Morris Minor, A.J. Cox of Shaftesbury; Morris Minor Traveller, C. Howe. The cars are in the yard at the rear of South Lynn. Left to right: Jack Simpson (sales manager), Ted Stickland (managing director), Anthony Stickland, Peter Crocker, Ian Stickland.

(Opposite)
The staff of Stickland's, 1921. Mr Jack Stickland was keen to obtain a Ford main dealership and set off to the Ford factory at Manchester to bargain for it. Realizing from the negotiations that they would need proof of the company's ability and commitment, he telephoned back with instructions to assemble all the staff and all available Ford vehicles for a photograph. The lettering was hastily painted on the door. The picture was taken and posted off to Manchester. The stunt was successful and a main dealership was granted.

A party for Stickland's staff to celebrate the completion of their new workshop, before it was soiled, 30 December 1960. Back row, left to right: Bob England, Jock MacQueen, Bill Green, Les Lampard, Jack Mead, Bob Lydford, John Cox, Fred Burt, Michael Mills, Stan Clark, John Garrett, Michael Waterhouse. Centre row, left to right: Jack Simpson, Ted Crocker, Wilfred Stevens, 'Duchy' Martin, George Jaggard, Doreen White, Tony Richens, Pam Hillier, Anthony Stickland, Brian Flower, Les Trim, Ted Howe, Michael Rawlings, 'Mot' Grey. Front row, left to right: Harold Bealing, Jack Miles, Ralph Crocker (managing director), Molly Stickland (director), Molly Crocker (director), John Pickford, David Lane, George Kite. Ironmongery, office, car sales, stores, workshop, paintshop and plumbing departments are represented.

SECTION FIVE

Notable Events

The uncrowned Queen visits Gillingham, 1952. Far left: Mr E. Batho (chairman of the Parish Council). Her Majesty is receiving a bouquet from Betty King who was the youngest girl at the Modern School. Far right: Isobel Case (head girl at the Grammar School). Among other engagements, the Queen called at Sandley Stud where her horses were bred. It was thirty-eight years before she made another official visit to Gillingham.

The visit of Gypsy Smith, 1939. Gypsy Smith (centre in the trilby) was an itinerant Methodist lay preacher who drew large congregations to his addresses. The pastor of the day, the Revd T. Bates, is standing on the right with his back to the gate.

After his arrival by train, Gladstone toured the district in support of the local Liberal candidate for the general election, *c.* 1885. Despite the crowds here in Newbury, there is only one policeman in sight. It is interesting to note that at this time the hotel in the background was called the Railway Hotel, no doubt to give the impression to people answering adverts that it was nearer to the station than it was. By the turn of the century the hotel was renamed the Royal, which it remains today.

(Opposite)
A dramatic accident on Phoenix Corner, August 1928. A Pickford's removal lorry ran out of control from the Wyke direction and failed to negotiate the bend into the High Street. It crashed into the shopfront of the London Central Meat Company. Fortunately no one was seriously hurt, but the butchers shop needed extensive repairs. St Mary's church gate can be seen between the buildings.

Devastation at Bourton caused by the bursting of the dam at Gasper. In the early hours of 29 June 1917, a torrential rainstorm caused considerable damage in the Stour Valley. Bourton was the first settlement in line when the dam burst. Bourton Foundry received extensive damage to its workshops and offices and 300 tons of coal in the yard were swept away, most never to be seen again! The man standing by the parapet (above) is Mr Fricker. Two views of the same bridge.

The bridge in Milton on Stour the same day. The *Western Gazette* reported that the rush of water was so great at Milton that the three-span bridge over the stream near the residence of Mr Kaine was destroyed. His home was flooded, and some of his poultry and a pig were lost.

When the floodwaters reached Gillingham they swept through the grounds and lower floor of the Plank House Red Cross Hospital. Miraculously, no staff or patients were drowned, even though at its height at 2 a.m. the water was a four-foot-deep torrent. This was the scene on the morning after in Wyke Street. Plank house is on the left.

The dedication of the war memorial, 18 November 1920. Large crowds turned out to watch the Earl of Shaftesbury perform the unveiling. In order to continue with the annual remembrance parade without causing chaos to the ever-increasing traffic, the memorial was moved to the rear of the adjacent car park in 1983.

A remembrance service before the memorial was moved, 9 November 1952. Revd Seager took the service and the bugler was Charles Howe.

The centrepiece exhibit in Gillingham Museum. This is an ornately carved wheelbarrow complete with solid silver spade, used to turn the first turf of the Salisbury and Yeovil railway on 3 April 1856. The exhibit was presented to Gillingham Museum by Yeovil Museum when it first opened in 1958. The Local History Society officers are, left to right: Alfie Davis, Colonel Wallis (the museum's prime mover and first curator), Reginald Shute.

Yeoman Warder John Webber visits Gillingham, Jubilee Day 1977. John, who was a Gillingham man, was presented with a Gillingham Silver Jubilee mug by Mrs Agnes Flower.

The town gets its own flag, 1966. 'Dinger' Bell raising the flag that he presented to the people and town of Gillingham. 'Dinger', who worked all his life at Matthews Brewery and distinguished himself by falling in to a beer vat, was a great character who was liked by all who met him. He 'gave his all' for the town, especially in support of the football team. The majority of the people witnessing the event were parish councillors. Left to right: Jack Burtt, Reg Shute, Herbert Green, Alfie Davis, Mrs J. Burtt, Squadron Leader Roupell, Bert Crocker, Phil Woodcock, Peter Webber, Bill Andrews, Eddie Batho, Don Mildenhall. (*Western Gazette*)

SECTION SIX

Sport and Leisure

The Hunt proceeding through Wyke having met at the Square, *c*. 1920. The two cottages (left of centre) were demolished in the 1930s and a tennis court made for the owners of Broadleigh, the house in the background. A bungalow now occupies the site.

Gillingham Football Club, 1897/8. The football ground was at Chantry Field. This group was in front of the railway bridge. Back row, left to right: J. Townsend (referee), F. Norris (Hon secretary), S. Hayter, A. Bridle, G. Atkinson (captain), W. King, S. Stone, A. Barnes (linesman). Front row, left to right: W. Senior, E. Stickland, S. Green, G. Burrington, W. Stead, E. Harris.

Young supporters for Gillingham football team's Cup match, 1967. The game was against Blandford and the home team lost 1–0. Even so the pitch was surrounded with cheering crowds. Left to right: Dennis Knox, Alan Doggrell, Steven Dardini, Alan Dunning, Graham Lloyd, Ian Drewitt, Peter Thick, Andrew Wilcox, Duncan King, Graham Crockford, Bill Palmer, Mike Lloyd, Steven Dunning.

Gillingham in action, September 1968. George Osborne (far left) is awaiting a pass from Len Arney. This time the team beat Hamworthy 5–1.

Fancy dress football match held on the Grammar School pitch, 1915. The match was held in aid of the Red Cross. Left to right: H. Stevens, P. Slade, ? Harding, F. Neville, C. Woodcock, G.E. Jukes, A. Jaggard, T. Foot, A Myall, ? Harding, S. Kite, ? Stokes. The building behind the goal was the police station and courtroom.

Another of the football teams functioning in 1918 was the St Mary's team. Front row, one from left: Bill Slade (the museum's curator from 1962 until 1977 and also a celebrated local historian).

A cricket tournament in Chantry Fields, 22 June 1907. Before the recreation ground in Hardings Lane was opened in 1926, many of the town's sport and other outdoor activities took place in Chantry Fields. These were still used for farming and therefore did not provide an ideal surface, but the surroundings were pleasant.

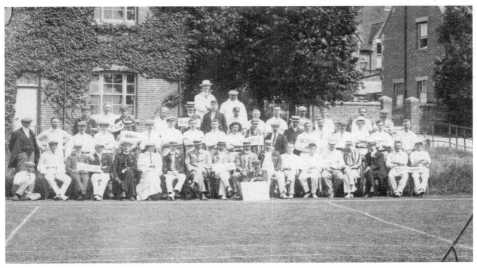

A three-a-side cricket tournament at the Grammar School, summer 1908. Teams from Gillingham, Thorngrove, Tisbury, Inwood, Mere, Sturminster, Stour, Wincanton, Stourton, Shaftesbury and Milborne Port were in action.

Gillingham Bowls Club, *c.* 1931. The interest is as much in the players' professions as the bowls. Back row, left to right: Ernest Berry (photographer, who almost certainly took this picture by delayed action or long lead), -?-, Mr Millard, Reg Bracher (undertaker and furnisher), Bill Wedlake (manager at the Town Mills), H. Godwin (auctioneer), D. Brown (manager of Oake, Woods and Company), C. Bariter, Mr Nicholson (printer). Centre row, left to right: J. Barnett (jeweller and optician), Mr Hopkins, C. Hayden, Mr Chaulkey, Mr Ashman, Ted Willis (agricultural representative – he's not paying attention!), Bill Hughes (baker), Alfie Beaton, Mr Scovill (Beaton and Scovill's outfitters), A. Davis (parish clerk). Front row, left to right: Mr Farrand, G. Blandford Matthews (G.B. Matthews Brewery), Ernest Martin (Hudson and Martin), Mr E. Ashman.

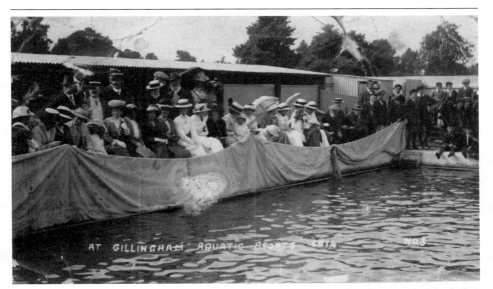

Aquatic sports at the Grammar School pool, soon after its opening in 1912. The ladies were well protected with an anti-splash tarpaulin.

Gillingham Water Polo Team, 1922. They played at the Grammar School Swimming Pool. The badge in the background is for the Gillingham Swimming Club. Back row, left to right: W. Codd, W. Scott, R. Balch, G. Newbury (trainer). Middle row: H. Philips, E. Tolley, P. Ridgley. Front row, left to right: N. Brown, W. Slade (captain), E. Cowling.

Sparring under the railway arch at Chantry, 1890s. The reason for this horseplay is not known. The arch was adjacent to the football field as well as being the route of one of the best-used footpaths.

Sailing on the Stour at Gillingham. If this was not the title inscribed on the negative, this might have been anywhere except Gillingham. Local opinion puts the scene at Eccliffe. This is backed by the evidence that other negatives found in the same batch by Edgar Samways were also taken there.

Opening Gillingham Recreation Ground. July, 1926

Opening of the Recreation Ground, July 1926. After much campaigning an official recreation ground was made in a field purchased from the Allard family of Lodden Farm. The rain did its very worst to ruin the day. This ground at Hardings Lane is still in use today.

The fair in Victoria Road, 1941. At this time the fair was not usually open for business as Coles fair is laid up for the war. The Recreation Ground is in the background. The lower shelter was dismantled in the early 1960s after much vandalism.

Gillingham Town Band, 1914. The town has always been blessed with a band to be proud of, probably never more so than in recent years under the dirdctorship of Fred Tranter. Back row, left to right: W. Wadman, A. Bridle, J. Williams, F. Ridout, C. Francis, H. Flower, C. Howe, B. Flower. Front row: E. Caesar, A. Flower, G. Harris (bandmaster), H. Harris, J. Wiles, E. Lodge.

The carnival barrel organ at the hospital carnival, 1908. This organ formed the centrepiece of fund raising for the various carnivals in the town for many years. It was always hoped that a permanent cottage hospital might be provided for Gillingham – we are still hoping!

The visit of the Southampton Police Band, 1912. The group of children in front include members of the Francis and Lush families. The boy in the boater and white smock is Eddie Bealing of the greengrocers.

The afternoon children's carnival procession, 1950. The interest is as much in the background as in the carnival itself. The cottages were demolished about two years later, and a hairdressers and wool shop were built which traded under the name of Dorothy Read. Later this shop became Anstee's.

Milmer Brown's popular decorated bicycle entry for Gillingham carnival, 1910. He is standing outside his home in St Martin's Square before setting out to the parade. His children here are Ronald and Stella. Milmer was sexton to St Mary's church for many years.

The 1790 Gillingham manual fire pump was made by Bristowe's of Whitechapel, and served the town exclusively until 1836 when a newer model was purchased by the Vestry Committee. It was, however, kept in working order as reserve until 1904 when a steam pump replaced them both. The original pump is shown here being used as a carnival float. It was stored in the Town Mill and Purn's Mill for many years until 1958 when the museum in Church Walk, where it has been on permanent exhibition, was opened.

A pageant to depict the making up of the Union Jack by St Mary's Scouts, 1949. The scouts are on the vicarage steps. Back row, left to right: David Fricker, Ray Warren, Eric Proudley. Centre row, left to right: Eric Smart, Bob Carter, Eric Scammell. Len Flower is sitting in front.

An outing assembled in Station Yard, ready to board a special train, probably to Weymouth, *c*. 1904. Until the middle 1950s the big event of the year was the annual Sunday School outing when the town emptied of most of its children. However, the other interest in this picture is provided by the buildings in the background. Left to right: the railway goods shed, sign boards for C.E. Maloney and Co., J.H. Rose 'furniture removals by road and rail', and Oake, Woods and Co. Ltd 'by Special Warrant to his Majesty the King').

Wyke Carnival, 1935. Few people in town now seem to be able to remember this event, but it is believed to have started in South Street and proceeded through Wyke to Wyke Recreation Ground which was to the rear of the Buffalo Inn. This recreation ground was on land belonging to the Matthews brewing family and at one time contained a shelter that could be turned to follow the sun. There was also a fine wrought iron gate with an arch above to celebrate the coronation of King George VI in 1937.

Hudson and Martin's company outing to Bournemouth in Stickland's charabanc and van, late summer 1919. Back row, left to right: T. Miles, W. Miles, E. Smart, F. Thick, W. Hull, B. Hull, S. Gray, M. Lush (slightly lower with trilby). Middle row, left to right: J. Vowles, W. Taylor, C. Wadman, B. Silcox, W. Hull, A. Webb. Front row, left to right: Ernest Martin, Hugh Martin, C. Compton, Harry Stevens (Stickland's staff, looking over shoulder), Hubert Harding (boy, who furnished all these names sixty-six years after the event), T. Foot (boater), E. Coats (boy), C. Maloney (bowler), E. Bowes, J. Smith (boy in dark suit), F. Foster (trilby), S. Stone, C. Gray, M. Read, T. Hull, C. Hayter (coat over arm), H. King, A. Wadman (boater), Harry Jaggard (Stickland's staff, standing by the garage door). The poster in the background advertises, 'Stalbridge Comrades of the Great War, Grand Fete, August 27th 1919.'

Compton Press staff outing just setting out from outside their printing works in the High Street, *c*. 1920. From left to right: George Lucas, Alby Arnold, Harry Lodge (arm on side), Arthur Wish, Clar Bealing (bowler hat), Erne Stokes (arm on side), Len Bird, Billy Green (at rear with trilby), Curly L. King (at side by horn), Charl Miles, -?-, Jack Westbrook (driver in light coat), Jim Herridge (behind windscreen in trilby), Bob England, Arthur Hull. The charabanc is a Garford and was first registered at the end of the First World War.

Gillingham Local History Society's first outing to the Pitt Rivers Museum at Farnham, 1954. Back row, left to right: Gillian Ralph, Mrs Ralph, -?-, Mrs Blandford Matthews, Mr Blandford Matthews, -?-, Colonel Wallis, Bill Slade, Alfie Davis, Sid Carter. Front row, left to right: -?-, Miss Manger, Mrs Hurley, Mrs Fea, Miss William, Mrs Wallis, -?-, Mrs Woodcock, Mrs Carter, Harry Flashman, Mrs Dean. It was through Mr Sid Carter's foresight that the original museum collection was saved for the town when the last of the Freame family died.

Gillingham and District Light Opera Company, 1934. The company was a breakaway group from the Gillingham Amateur Operatic Society. They were renowned for their Gilbert and Sullivan productions between the wars. This is a scene from *Mr Cinders*, which was performed at the Market Hall.

The Scout Pantomime, 1954. This was performed in the Vicarage Schoolroom. Left to right: Roger Mayo, Owen Dicker, Ken Warren, M. Amor, Wilf Davidson, John Bracher. The scripts were always written by the vicar, Revd E.L. Seager.

The Blackmore Vale Scouts leading a parade in the High Street, just prior to the First World War. The event was probably for a slate club or the Odd Fellows. The town band and fire brigade were behind. The Wilts and Dorset Bank was extended with another wing on the Methodist chapel side in 1919.

Dedicating the British Legion Standard in the Station Yard, 1929. In the background the milk train can be seen waiting to be loaded. The farmers that had contracted to sell their milk direct to a dairy in London or en route had to bring their churns in early to catch the 9 a.m. train. If they missed it the milk could still go on a later train but there was a price penalty.

SECTION SEVEN

Tracks and Trains

The heyday of the London and South Western Railway, 1905. A 4–4–0 engine, familiar in the early part of the century, has stopped on the downline. Apparently emerging from the engine's chimney is the windpump, which lifted the water from the well to the water tanks, situated on the upside beyond the footbridge. The downside water crane is in the right foreground.

Shunting horses at the station, *c.* 1915. The shunter is F. France and the boy is Jim Smart. The wagon below was probably shunted by this very team.

One of Maloney's coal wagons, as shown in a publicity photograph for the wagon builders, S.J. Claye Ltd of Long Eaton. Maloney's had a number of these, which were sent direct to the colliery to be loaded and then delivered to their siding at Gillingham station. J.H. Rose and Sons who later bought Maloney's coal business added these wagons to their own. When the railways were nationalized, these were taken over by British Railways.

The train that brought Prime Minister Gladstone to Gillingham. This decorated Adams 460 class engine was designed for the gradients on the Salisbury to Exeter line, and is standing at Gillingham's down platform (see p. 115).

A fine bunch of station staff, 1925. Back row, left to right: Signalman Woodley, Porter Scammel, Porter Hoskins, Porter Belgin, Porter Coles. Middle row, left to right: Signalman Knight, Driver Hoskins, Porter Hooper, Weighbridge Operater Cull, Porter Stone, Driver Francis, Porter Hallet, Porter Mitchell, Porter Drew. Front row: Signalman Smart, Foreman Mirch, Clerk Tolley, Clerk Anderson, Station Master Lee, Clerk Cull, Clerk Lilley, Clerk Martin.

A busy goods yard, 1953. The goods office was being rebuilt in the middle distance. Coal, cattle and general goods wagons are in the sidings.

British Railways Standard class four engine emerges from the Sandley Tunnel with the Salisbury to Yeovil local train, 1964. This was the last year of normal steam working.

The Down Shelter, 1953. This was demolished in 1987 and the signal box beyond was replaced with a modern building ten yards further on in the 1960s.

The eastern end of Sandley Tunnel, early 1930s. A gang is clearing up after a landslip which had blocked the line.

The railway viaduct under repair, 1899. Although this viaduct gave the appearance of being a robust and soundly constructed edifice, the foundations on clay gave cause for frequent maintenance. Here only one tie bar is in place, but now there are rail sections bracing a larger area.

The quarry face excavator at Gillingham Pottery, Brick and Tile clay pits, with a locomotive waiting to pick up loaded wagons. Railway enthusiasts will note the different gauge rails.

Clay was brought to the brickworks in these wagons. The passing loop is in the foreground. The loaded wagons were winched up the incline in the left background and tipped.

These wagons, connected to the winch cable, are waiting to be hauled up the incline. Bert Francis is standing by.

In Uniform

The fire brigade lined up outside the School Lane Fire Station, 1935. Back row, left to right: J. Hine, T. Hayden, T. Flower, A. Sheppard, A. Belgin. Centre row, left to right: E. Hine (driver), T. Hillier, J. Webber, H. Luffman, D. Tucker. Front row, left to right: H. Harris (captain), J. Burtt (seated), J. Case (seated on right), L. Brown. Some of their helmets are on display in the museum. The fire engine is a Lincoln.

This is believed to be the oldest known photograph of Gillingham. It was taken in the garden of the Chantry, Commonmead Lane and was presented 'By the members of the 11th Dorset Rifle Volunteers to Lieutenant R.S. Freame on resigning his command of the Corps, December 1864.' Robert Sadler Freame was one of the first to enroll in 1860 and was its first commanding officer.

Doctors, nurses and other staff of Plank House Red Cross Hospital, First World War. Seated row, fifth from left is Dr Farnfield; next to him is Mrs Farnfield (sister in charge, with white armband), and far right is Miss Freame. At the end of the war Mrs Farnfield was decorated by Queen Alexandra with the Royal Red Cross.

The Corps of Volunteer Ambulance Drivers, comprised of people from all walks of life who gave their services in the First World War. They transported the wounded servicemen, largely soldiers from the French battlefields, who arrived by train, to local temporary hospitals in Gillingham and Mere.

Camp for the 4th Dorset Territorial Army. Andrew McQueen is on the motor cycle and Charlie Lush is in the sidecar. Andrew McQueen spent twelve years in the Territorials before the Second World War. Charlie Lush was a well-known figure who loved to entertain with the mouth organ.

The funeral of Robert Coward, the longest-surviving soldier of the Crimean War, 3 May 1923. The soldiers and gun carriage were brought from Larkhill for the occasion. Robert Coward was the second in a family of fourteen children and had lived in Gillingham for the greater part of his ninety-two years. His father fought at the battle of Waterloo.

The telegraph boy. Fred Brown proudly posing in smart uniform in Edwardian times.

Gillingham post office staff, 1926. Back row, left to right: Mr Newbury, Charles Stickland, Jack King, Reg Hunt, Mr Smith. Centre row, left to right: Mr Snow (caretaker), Gerald Flower (telegram boy), Mr Young, Mr Scammell, Mr Larcombe, Mr Drewitt. Front row, left to right: Miss Lush, Miss Lovelace, -?-, Mr Richardson (postmaster), Miss Down, Mr Stevens, -?-.

Kenneth Norman Read in RAF uniform, 1941. Aged 21, he is standing on the old railway bridge while on leave. His family kept the bicycle shop nearby (see p. 32). Sadly he was a casualty of the Second World War. His aircraft was lost in action on the night of 4/5 of July 1944.

The VAD detachment of the Second World War on the vicarage lawn. Back row, left to right: Mrs Sims, Mrs Samways, Miss Head. Next row, left to right: Mrs Buckley, Mrs Andrews, Mrs J. Martin, Miss Coombs, Mrs Baxter, Mrs Davies, Mrs Bracher, Mrs Baxter, Mrs Alexander, Miss Manger. Seated row, left to right: Mrs Welsman, Nurse Read, Mrs Warren, Mrs Matthews, Dr Alexander, Nurse Cox, Miss Bishop. Front row, left to right: Mrs Hayden, Mrs Lodge, Mrs Knott, Mrs Lanham.

Gillingham's Home Guard, 1945. Back row, left to right: N. Dunning, G. Martin, Bob Ridout, Fred White, Frank Warr, ? Jefferey, J. Fry, F. Clark, Mot Grey, R. Gatehouse, -?-, G. Watts, A. Hall, G. Cox. Next row, left to right: -?-, M. Holland, R. Watts, Owen Green, Keith Burton, Cecil Wadman, V. Rigler, R. Standerwick, R. Ridout, T. Johnson, S. Toogood, Hubert Harding, E. Luffman. Seated row, left to right: A. Thompson, Ralph Crocker, ? Rammel, G. Gray, Cecil Everitt, R. Lock, R. Jukes, R. Jefford, ? Lee, Billy Green, R. Brown, ? Smith, Les Dunning, George Joyce. Front row, left to right: F. Biles, ? Brine, H. Case, W. Bealing, Dick Pike, ? Chambers. The drill hall (now the Youth Centre) was used for parades.

The Civil Defence First Aid Group of the Second World War, at the rear of Eden Shute's premises, New Road, November 1942. Back row, left to right: Peggy Jukes, Ivy Hiscock (now Lloyd), Ray Spragg, Revd Treasure, Stewart Strange, Stan Newport, Freda Howe (now Hull), Phyllis Newport. Middle row, left to right: Mrs Ball, Doris Johnston, Miss Down, Joan Aplin, Mrs Wadman, Joy Webb, Barbara Bracher, Molly Goodson (now Griffiths), Nona Gray (now Phillips), Gwen Hillier, Mrs Roberts. Front row, left to right: Hilda Harrison (now Collier), Mrs Edwards, Mrs Deane, Mrs Dickenson, Mrs Buckley, Dr Alexander, Miss Bishop, Mrs Beaton, Mrs Jaggard, Mrs Scovill, Miss Coombs.

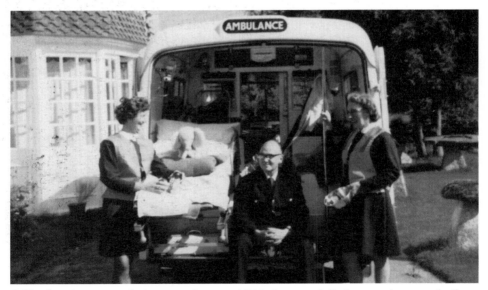

Gillingham's own ambulance and crew, 1975. Later a full time station was built at Shaftesbury to cover the whole area. Left to right: Mary Jacobs, Doug Francis, Betty Ridout.

SECTION NINE
Bird's Eye View

The Station Road sawmills of Hudson and Martin, *c.* 1925. The River Stour is at the bottom and Station Road is at the top. The field at the top was used for fairs and was owned by the Braddick family. The largest building in Buckingham Road (left) was until 1934 the town's main cinema and is now the Coronation Club. The long buildings, also in Buckingham Road, were John Jeffrey's cattle market with premises both sides of the road where Baker's Garage now stands.

Newbury from the west. The junction with Station Road and the High Street is at centre bottom with the road leading away to join Shaftesbury Road at top left. Victoria Road at centre left led to a paddock which is now the continuation of the road. Virtually all of the trees on the town side of the railway have gone. This was one of a series of aerial pictures taken in the 1920s. Only three of these are in the museum's collection; all of them are reproduced in this book.

(Opposite, bottom)
Bay, Lodbourne and Peacemarsh from a north-easterly direction, 1967. The prominent feature is Fairey Crescent. The other major group of houses is the Y shape of Coronation Road and Deweys Way. At top left the L-shaped field is part of Barnaby Mead. The first stage of Shreen Way is between Fairey Crescent and the River Shreen. All of the fields at the bottom are now covered by the continuation of Shreen Way, Brookside, Broadacres, Highgrove, Blacklawn, Claremont Avenue, Bourne Way, Cordery Gardens, Downsview Drive, Honeyfields plus many secondary addresses. Saxons Mead is in the course of construction at centre right and west of Peacemarsh, which runs from centre right to the Lodbourne junction. Queen Street is top left. Bay Road starts at the Lodbourne junction, where the entrance to Lodbourne Farm is also to be found, and proceeds to the bottom left corner. The other green field which is also now under houses is the Wessex Way development near the top right corner.

High Street from the church tower before the cinema was built, early 1930s. The houses in the middle distance at top right are in Buckingham Road.

Queen Street from the church tower, 1906. Tower House is just left of centre and the recently built St Martin's House is in the right foreground. The rise in the background is Bowridge Hill. The writer of this postcard on a cycling tour was 'feeling very comfortable' in the Phoenix Hotel and wrote, 'Gillingham is a nice quiet pretty place.'

Looking down on the lower town, 1925. The Victorian cemetery is in the foreground. First used in 1861, it was filled by the turn of the century when the present burial ground was established. The drill hall, which is now the Youth Centre, had not yet been built in the open space at the right. The gasholders of the Gillingham Gas, Light and Coke company, and St Mary's church, are near the top right. The cottage on the junction of Turners Lane and Cemetery Road was demolished around 1935. By that time the orchard at the bottom left had become Orchard Road.

Wyke and Commonmead Lane, 1967. Many of these fields were about to lose their turf to housing developments. The road from bottom left to approximately the centre among the trees is Wyke Road, and the lane from centre right to a converging point is Commonmead Lane. The fields to the left of Wyke Road are occupied by Briar Close, Hawthorn Avenue (and others). The larger field to the right of the road has an estate fed by Milestone Way. The new Wyke Primary School is in the top right of the same field, and the round water storage tank in the centre is now part of the school's playing field. The two smaller paddocks adjoining incorporate Broad Robin, and the big curved field is now Maple Way with Freame Way at bottom right and Laburnum Way just above. Above (south of) Commonmead Lane are Stour Meadows and Stour Gardens, with Chantry Fields beyond.

ACKNOWLEDGEMENTS

My special thanks go to Lyn Light, Hon Curator of Gillingham Museum, who has helped sort out and, worse still, put away the hundreds of photographs from the museum collection that we have sifted through; David Lloyd, whose guidance, research and checking of my work has helped no end; Merelina Ross for her great help with some of the village pictures and information; my very understanding wife, Glynis, who had to undertake the lion's share of the gardening during the spring and summer that this book absorbed of my spare time; and, not to be forgotten, my daughter Lianne, who gave practical assistance by way of typing, sorting and pasting up of the work.

The following is a list of many of the people who have loaned photographs, helped put names to faces and supplied other information, and without whose help this book might never have happened.

Bill Budden • Margaret Burton • Tom Carrick • Mrs Violet Cockerell
Tony Coombes • Mrs J. Crabtree • Ralph Crocker (my father) • Peter Daniels
Mrs Winifred Dowding • East Stour WI • John Flashman • Elizabeth Fricker
Herbert Green • Owen Green • Molly Griffiths • Arnold Hallett
Hubert Harding • Rachel Harris • Ronald Harris • Pat Hillier • Gordon Hine
Colin Hoare • Barbara Howe • Harry Hunt • Mrs Gladys Isaacs • Jean Joyce
Peter Jukes • Tony Lampard • Trustees of Langham church • Herbie Light
Eileen McQueen • Chris Marsh • Revd John McNeish • Roger Mayo
Michael Mills • Mary Morse • Edith Myall • Lorna Perrin • Michael Pike
Dr Michael Plaxton • Monica Rhodes • Janet Robson • Michael Rose
Tim Rose • Den Sharp • Silton WI • Rex Standerwick • Frank Stokes
Jack Suter • Dr Geoffrey Tapper • Mr and Mrs M. Tonkin • Victor Toogood
Mrs B. Turvey • Joe Wareham • David Webber • Mrs P Woodcock
Sam Woodcock.

Thank you also to the dozens of people of the town and area who are not mentioned but have helped me on my way with my enquiries, or have given pictures to the museum, recently or in past years.

Peter Crocker, 1992